D1117228

A Robbie Reader

Mt. Vesuvius and the Destruction of Pompeii, A.D. 79

Russell Roberts

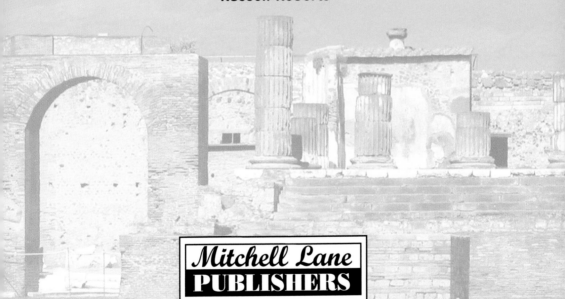

Mitchell Lane
PUBLISHERS

P.O. Box 196
Hockessin, Delaware 19707
Visit us on the web: www.mitchelllane.com
Comments? email us: mitchelllane@mitchelllane.com

Mitchell Lane PUBLISHERS

Printing   2   3   4   5   6   7   8   9

A Robbie Reader/Natural Disasters

The Ancient Mystery of Easter Island
The Bermuda Triangle, 1945
Bubonic Plague
Earthquake in Loma Prieta, California, 1989
The Fury of Hurricane Andrew, 1992
Hurricane Katrina, 2005
The Lost Continent of Atlantis
Mt. Vesuvius and the Destruction of Pompeii, A.D. 79
Mudslide in La Conchita, California, 2005
Tsunami Disaster in Indonesia, 2004
Where Did All the Dinosaurs Go?

Library of Congress Cataloging-in-Publication Data
Roberts, Russell, 1953 –
    Mt. Vesuvius and the destruction of Pompeii/by Russell Roberts.
        p. cm. – (A Robbie Reader) (Natural disasters – what can we learn?)
    Includes bibliographical references and index.
    ISBN 1-58415-419-5 (lib. bd.)
    1. Pompeii (Extinct city) – Juvenile literature. 2. Vesuvius (Italy) – Eruption, 79 – Juvenile literature. I. Title. II. Series. III. Series: Natural disasters – what can we learn?
    DG70. P7R63 2005
    937'.7 – dc22
                                                                                                    2005009697
ISBN-10: 1-58415-419-5   ISBN-13: 9781584154198

ABOUT THE AUTHOR: Russell Roberts has written and published over 35 books for adults and children on a variety of subjects, including baseball, memory power, business, New Jersey history, and travel. He has also written numerous books for Mitchell Lane, including *Pedro Menendez de Aviles, Philo Farnsworth Invents TV, Robert Goddard, Bernardo de Galvez,* and *Where Did the Dinosaurs Go?* He lives in Bordentown, New Jersey, with his family and a fat, fuzzy, and crafty calico cat named Rusti.

PHOTO CREDITS: Cover, pp. 1, 4, 6 – Barbara Marvis; p. 8 – USGS/Lyn Topinka; p. 10 – Andrea Pickens, p. 13 – USGS/Lyn Topinka; p. 14 – Jamie Kondrchek; p. 17 – Barbara Marvis; p. 18 – Andrea Pickens; p. 20 – Barbara Marvis; p. 23 – John Mcconnico/Associated Press; pp. 24, 26 – Barbara Marvis

PUBLISHER'S NOTE: The following story has been thoroughly researched and to the best of our knowledge represents factual events. While every possible effort has been made to ensure accuracy, the publisher will not assume liability for damages caused by inaccuracies in the data, and makes no warranty on the accuracy of the information contained herein.

TABLE OF CONTENTS

Words in **bold** type can be found in the glossary.

The inside of the Basilica at Pompeii. The Basilica was the largest building in the city. Business and legal matters were conducted there.

LUNCHTIME

It is lunchtime on August 24 in A.D. 79. A family gets ready to eat. Slaves bring their food. But the family will never eat it.

The family lives in the city of Pompeii (pom-PAY). Pompeii is part of the **Roman Empire**. Rome is very powerful and controls many other countries.

Pompeii is a busy city of 20,000 people. It is on the Bay of Naples in southern Italy, about 150 miles south of Rome. It has a pleasant climate, and people go there for vacation. Pottery and glass are made in Pompeii. So is cloth for clothing. There are

The remains of a bakery in Pompeii. The eruption happened so quickly that some loaves of bread were left baking.

bakeries and laundries. People buy food in a large outdoor market. They watch plays in theaters and pray to gods in temples.

Pompeii is a very modern city for the time. Gutters in the street carry away sewage. Pipes bring in fresh water. There are three public baths so the people can stay clean.

Several miles away is a mountain. It is called Vesuvius (vuh-SOO-vee-us). People hunt in its woods. They plant fruit orchards on its slopes. Vesuvius seems like a friendly neighbor.

It is not. Vesuvius is actually a **volcano** (vahl-KAY-no). Nobody in Pompeii knows that. It has not erupted for over one thousand years. But that does not mean it cannot erupt again.

Early in August of A.D. 79, unusual things begin happening. Several tremors (TREH-murs) occur. Tremors are small vibrations of the earth. Some wells dry up. On August 20 there is a bigger earthquake. Birds get quiet.

In Washington State in 1980, Mount St. Helens erupted. When Mt. Vesuvius erupted, it might have looked a lot like this.

Horses and cattle are excited. These are signs that Vesuvius is about to erupt.

But nothing seems unusual at lunchtime on August 24. Just as the food is served to the family, there is a loud roar. Vesuvius is erupting! Hot rocks and gases from the volcano shoot 17 miles into the air.

The family runs outside. An angry black cloud covers the sun. It is dark as night. Earthquakes shake the ground. Vesuvius is spitting fire.

Many people are running out of Pompeii. The family runs, too. They leave behind their house and all their possessions. The road is crowded and dark. Everyone is scared.

The family is lucky. They escape unharmed. Others are not so lucky. They decide to stay and take shelter in their homes. They think they are safe.

They are wrong.

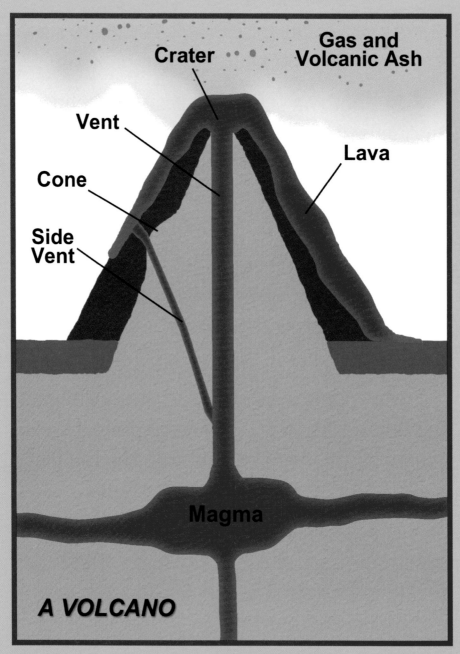

Crater

Gas and Volcanic Ash

Vent

Lava

Cone

Side Vent

Magma

A VOLCANO

When a volcano erupts, hot magma from below Earth's surface rises through the vent in the volcano cone. At the surface, magma is called lava. Gas and ash from the eruption can travel miles into the sky. Winds can spread the gas and ash thousands of miles, even across oceans.

VOLCANOES

What is a volcano?

A volcano is a high hill or mountain with a hole at its **summit** (SUH-mut). The hole lets hot gases and **magma** (MAG-muh) escape from deep inside Earth. Magma is melted rock. Magma that flows to the surface is called **lava** (LAH-vuh). When lava meets air, it cools and gets hard. Each time lava comes out and hardens, it makes the volcano bigger.

Sometimes magma hardens inside the volcano. It blocks anything from escaping. It is like a cork. Pressure builds up over time. Finally the pressure gets too great. It blows the cork out, and the volcano erupts.

There are volcanoes all over the world. Many are like Vesuvius. They are on land and can easily be seen. Others are under the oceans. The country of Indonesia in Southeast Asia has the most volcanoes.

Volcanoes do some good things. They make rich soil for growing crops. They supply minerals like zinc and copper. They put water vapor into the air.

But eruptions are usually deadly.

There have been many famous volcanic eruptions. In 1815 in Indonesia, a volcano called Tambora erupted. It was one of the biggest eruptions in history. Tons of dust and gas shot into the sky. The eruption even changed the weather. It rained where it usually did not. It did not rain where it usually did. In the United States, the dust and gas made it cold in the summer. Because of this, 1816 was called "the year without a summer." Crops and animals died. New England had frost in July and August.

Krakatau (krah-kuh-TAU) was another big eruption. It occurred in 1883. Krakatau is also in Indonesia. The eruption created giant waves called tsunamis (soo-NAH-meez). They killed nearly 40,000 people.

Mount St. Helens is a volcano in Washington State. It erupted on May 18, 1980. Sixty-four people were killed, and the mountain lost more than one thousand feet of its height.

When Mount St. Helens erupted, the blast knocked over these huge trees. Then volcanic ash covered them.

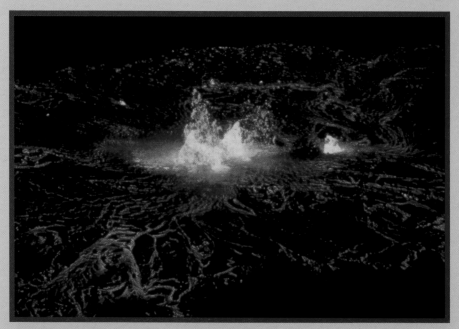

Magma is melted rock under Earth's surface.

Lava is magma that flows from a volcano to Earth's surface.

EYEWITNESS

Thirty minutes after Vesuvius erupts, rocks begin falling from the sky. It is like rain. Most are **pumice** (PUH-miss). Pumice has many tiny holes. It is so light that it floats. But some of the rocks are heavy enough to kill. Some people tie pillows on their heads for protection.

The eruption hurts animals, too. Birds are killed and fall to the ground. Ash from Vesuvius falls into the ocean. It mixes with the water. The water turns pasty and mushy. Fish die and wash ashore.

Pumice and ash keep falling on Pompeii. Every hour six more inches fall. It piles up on roofs. Some people are killed as their roofs collapse. Other people are trapped inside their homes when pumice blocks the doors. The eruption causes earthquakes, which knock over oil lamps. The hot oil starts fires.

Twelve miles away a man watches Vesuvius erupt. His name is Pliny (PLY-nee) the Elder. He is across the Bay of Naples at a naval base called Misenum (mih-SEE-num). Pliny the Elder is a famous navy commander and science expert. He wants to rescue people. He orders a boat to take him to Pompeii.

His teenage nephew, named Pliny the Younger, is visiting him. He does not go with his uncle. Later he writes about the eruption. That is how we know what happened. Young Pliny thinks the whole world is dying. He says that the cloud coming out of Vesuvius looks like a spreading tree.

Mt. Vesuvius looms in the background behind Pompeii, a constant reminder of the day when it erupted and destroyed the city.

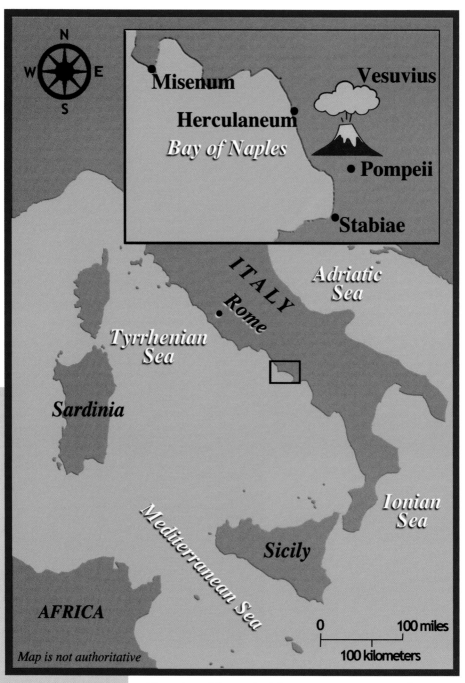

Map is not authoritative

Pliny the Elder sailed from Misenum toward Pompeii, hoping to rescue people. He landed in Stabiae.

Pliny the Elder takes his boat toward the eruption. But he cannot land. The water is choked with ash and pumice. Pliny instead lands four miles away at a town called Stabiae (STAY-bee-eye). He has friends there. His friends are worried and Pliny tries to calm them. He goes to sleep to show them everything is all right.

The next morning Pliny goes outside. Ash from Vesuvius makes it dark as night. Suddenly Pliny falls down dead. He has choked on fumes.

Pliny the Younger escapes from Misenum. Many others run away too. The road is filled with scared people. They are calling to each other. They cannot see in the darkness.

Plaster was poured into the molds left by people's bodies in the ruins of Pompeii. They were killed so quickly that even today, almost 2,000 years later, scientists know exactly what the people were doing at the moment they died.

TRAPPED

After eight hours, Vesuvius is still erupting. Every second, more than 100,000 tons of material are spewed from the volcano. The ash and rock make the air very dry. People choke.

Night falls. Lightning dances around the volcano. It is pretty. It is also scary.

Then deadly clouds begin sliding down the side of Vesuvius. These are called **avalanches** (AA-vuh-lan-chez). The clouds are made up of ash, gas, and rock. The ash and gas travel faster. They go 100 miles per hour, faster than cars on a highway. The rocks move more slowly. They are very hot, some over 1,000 degrees Fahrenheit.

The avalanche sweeps into a town called Herculaneum (her-kyoo-LAH-nee-um). It is 10 miles from Vesuvius. Many people there have run to the beach. They hope that boats will rescue them. But no boats come. Then the avalanche hits. It kills everyone instantly. Five more avalanches strike Herculaneum and bury the town under 65 feet of ash and rock.

So far no avalanches have struck Pompeii. But that is about to change.

At about the time Pliny the Elder walks outside in Stabiae, Vesuvius has been erupting for 17 hours. Many tons of ash, rock, and pumice have fallen on Pompeii. Two thousand people remain in the city. Many hide inside. Some try to go out. Everyone wonders when the eruption will stop.

Then an avalanche hits. There is no time to escape. Everyone left in Pompeii is killed. A woman dies holding her jewels. A man dies trying to cover the mouth of a woman who is going to have a baby. A mule driver dies crouched against a wall.

Ash covers everything in Pompeii. It settles like giant gray snowdrifts.

Volcanic rock and ash lie 10 feet deep over a city on Montserrat, an island in the Caribbean Sea. The volcano in the background, Soufrière (soo-free-AIR), erupted in 1995. It spewed gas and ash for years. Unlike the people near Vesuvius, the people in this city had time to escape.

Some of the paintings in Pompeii are still bright and colorful. Others were damaged and had to be restored.

REDISCOVERY

After 19 hours, Vesuvius stops erupting. The dark clouds above the volcano blow away. The sun comes out. Pompeii has disappeared. It is buried under ash and rock that are 25 feet deep in some places.

Some people return. They try to dig down to their homes, hoping to get things from them. It is dangerous to dig because poisonous gas is trapped under the ashes. The people stop digging. During the following centuries, Vesuvius erupts several more times. Pompeii is buried even deeper. Slowly people forget about the city.

In 1699, Pompeii is rediscovered. People begin **excavating** (EKS-cuh-vay-ting) it in 1748. It is a city frozen in time. You can still see writing on the walls. You can still see the

Since excavations began in 1748, tourists have flocked to see the city that was frozen in time. Every day, millions of people from around the world visit the ancient city of Pompeii.

color of paintings. You can still see bread that had been baking in ovens.

The bodies of those killed have turned to dust. But the bodies left perfect shapes in the hardened ash. When plaster is poured into the shapes, it makes an exact statue of the person. The statues show what people were doing when they died.

The eruption of Mount Vesuvius in A.D. 79 must have been horrifying. Yet this natural disaster has given us a gem today. Because the volcano buried the area so quickly and completely, we have a detailed picture of how people lived almost 2,000 years ago.

Vesuvius has erupted over 100 times since 79. None of the eruptions was as bad as the one that destroyed Pompeii. The last time it erupted was in 1944.

CHRONOLOGY

6th century B.C.	Pompeii is founded.
80 B.C.	Pompeii becomes a Roman city.
A.D. 62	A major earthquake causes widespread damage in Pompeii.
A.D. 79	

	Aug. 20	An earthquake shakes Pompeii.
	Aug. 24	Mt. Vesuvius erupts.
	Aug. 25	Herculaneum is buried around 1:00 A.M. Later in the day, an avalanche buries Pompeii.
	Aug. 26	Mt. Vesuvius stops erupting, but not for good.

1699	Pompeii is rediscovered.
1710	Well diggers discover Herculaneum.
1748	Excavations begin at Pompeii.
1845	The Vesuvian Observatory opens.
1944	Mt. Vesuvius erupts again, the most recent of over 100 eruptions since A.D. 79.
1995	Vesuvius National Park opens.

NOTABLE VOLCANIC ERUPTIONS SINCE 1600

Year	Volcano	Country
1631	Vesuvius	Italy
1741	Oshima	Japan
1783	Lakagigar	Iceland
1815	Tambora	Indonesia
1877	Cotopaxi	Ecuador
1883	Krakatau	Indonesia
1902	Mount Pelée	Martinique
1980	Mount St. Helens	United States
1982	El Chichón	Mexico
1986	Lake Nyos	Cameroon
1991–1996	Mount Pinatubo	Philippines

FIND OUT MORE

Books

Balit, Christina. *Escape from Pompeii*. New York: Henry Holt, 2003.

Humphrey, Kathryn Long. *Pompeii: Nightmare at Midday*. New York: Franklin Watts, 1990.

Kunhardt, Edith. *Pompeii—Buried Alive!* New York: Random House, 1987.

Seely, John, and Elizabeth Seely. *Pompeii and Herculaneum*. Chicago: Heinemann Library, 1992.

Tanaka, Shelley. *The Buried City of Pompeii*. New York: Hyperion Books, 2000.

Works Consulted

Amery, Colin, and Brian Curran Jr. *The Lost World of Pompeii*. Los Angeles: Getty Publications, 2002.

De Boer, Jelle Zeilinga, and Donald Theodore Sanders. *Volcanoes in Human History*. Princeton, New Jersey: Princeton University Press, 2002.

Giuntoli, Stefano. *Art and History of Pompeii*. Translated by Erika Pauli. Florence, Italy: Casa Editrice Boniche, 2004.

Vesuvio: The Story and Eruption of a Volcano. Translation by ATD Mailand. Kina Italy, no date.

Films

Pompeii, Buried Alive: Extraordinary Secrets of Ancient Pompeii Revealed. Produced by Multimedia Entertainment, Inc. and Filmroos, Inc. in association with A&E Network. New York: A&E Home Video; New York: Reader's Digest, 1995.

Pompeii: The Last Day. The Discovery Channel, Produced by the Discovery Channel and the BBC, 2003.

On the Internet

Mt. Vesuvius Webcam
  http://www.vesuvioinrete.it/e_webcam.htm

Vesuvius, Italy
  http://volcano.und.nodak.edu/vwdocs/volc_images/img_vesuvius.html

Pompeii: Vesuvius

    http://www.harcourtschool.com/activity/pompeii/pmpVesu.html

A.D. 79 Eruption of Mount Vesuvius, Italy

    http://vulcan.fis.uniroma3.it/vesuvio/79_eruption.html

Table of Notable Volcanic Disasters Since A.D. 1500

    http://volcanoes.usgs.gov/Hazards/Effects/Fatalities.html

Ancient Pompeii

    http://www.thehumorwriter.com/Kids_Corner_–_Original_Storie/
Ancient_Pompeii/ancient_pompeii.html

GLOSSARY

A.D.	a label used to indicate years that came after the birth of Jesus of Nazareth.
avalanche	(AA-vuh-lanch)—deadly clouds of ash, gas, and rock that slide down the slope of an erupting volcano.
excavating	(EKS-cuh-vay-ting)—exposing something to view by digging around it.
lava	(LAH-vuh)—magma that reaches Earth's surface.
magma	(MAG-muh)—molten rock below Earth's surface.
pumice	(PUH-miss)—a type of volcanic glass that has many holes, so it is lightweight.
Roman Empire	an important ancient civilization that controlled much of Europe and northern Africa.
summit	(SUH-mut)—the highest point of a mountain or hill.
volcano	(vahl-KAY-noe)—a high hill or mountain with a hole that allows hot gases and magma to escape to Earth's surface.

INDEX